THE FLYING SAUCERS

By ROLF TELANO, Tk., Com.

ILLUSTRATED

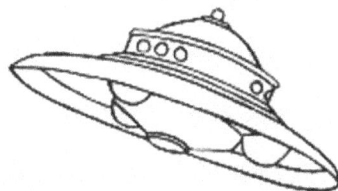

SAUCERIAN PUBLISHER

ISBN:978-1-955087-05-6

9 781955 087056

© 2022, Saucerian Publisher

PROLOGUE

It is generally a good idea to return to the classics in any genre. This also goes for UFO literature. Rereading a book, or reviewing old documents after ten or twenty years is a rewarding experience. You will discover new data and ideas you didn´t notice before. The reason, of course, is that you are, in many ways, not the same person reading the book the second or third time. Hopefully you have advanced in knowledge, experience, intellectual and spiritual discernment. A good starting point is to reread the contactee classics material of the 1960s, in order to understand the deeper mystery involved in what happened during that era.

During the dawn of the UFO age, three channelers or mediums significantly impacted ufology. Mark Probert, Ralph Holland (Rolf Telano), and Gerald Light (Dr. Kappa). One of the most influential contactees was Ralph Merridette Holland. On August 29, 1899, Holland was born and died on January 26, 1962), also known as Rolf Telano. He was an American contactee (particularly of a Venus Etherian priestess called Borealis Telano), medium, and ufo author. He designed a telepathic transmission device called Project Hermes (Resh-Mem-Heh) device that according to its creator is a "reproduction of an ancient communication instrument" (comparable to Richard Shaver's telaug) that could be used for mental communication with other living beings as well as "entities on other planes, if properly tuned. Holland reported that his circuit design for the device was based on information he had received from the spirit of Nikola Tesla.

Saucerian Publisher was founded to promote Flying Saucer, Paranormal, and the Occult books. Our vision is to preserve the legacy of literary history by reprinting editions of books that have already been exhausted or are difficult to obtain. Our goal is to help readers, educators, and researchers by bringing back original publications that are difficult to find at a reasonable price while preserving the legacy of universal knowledge. This title is an authentic reproduction of the original Telano's *The flying saucers.* It was initially published in 1952 as mimeographed manuscript for a very limited circulation. Then in 1963, Gray Baker published it as a 62 pages booklet. This book is a facsimile reproduction of the original printed text in shades of gray. Because this material is culturally important, we have made it available as part of our commitment to protect, preserve and promote knowledge in the world. **IMPORTANT,although we have attempted to maintain the integrity of the issues accurately, the present reproduction could have missing and blurred pages poor pictures due to the age of the original scanned copy. Because this material is culturally important, we have made it available as part of our commitment to protect, preserve and promote knowledge in the world.**

Editor
Saucerian Publisher, 2022

THE
FLYING SAUCERS

By ROLF TELANO, Tk., Com.

ILLUSTRATED

This edition is dedicated
To the Late
Meade Layne

INTRODUCTION

The year, 1952, was certainly a big one for the flying saucers.

Probably the largest concentration of sightings, many of them close, dramatic ones, took place in that year. It was the year that Florida scoutmaster, J. D. "Sonny" Desvergers, said he was burned by one, after he went into a thicket to investigate what he thought had been a plane crash. It was the year in which Bill Squyres, a radio entertainer of Station KOAM, Pittsburgh, Kansas, had a close brush with a 75-foot-long flying machine, which hovered close the ground and was encountered on his way to work -- obviously Case No. 12 in the "12 good sightings" listed in the Air Force's PROJECT BLUE BOOK SPECIAL REPORT No. 14.

In September of that year seven of my neighbors were scared almost out of their wits when they went to a hilltop at Flatwoods, W. Va., to view a "fallen meteor," and instead encountered the famed Flatwoods Monster.

It was the year in which George Adamski met a spaceman from Venus in a California desert.

If the year were a great one for saucerenthusiasts, mainly because of all the excitement going on, it was also a year in which intelligence, common sense, and level-headedness needed to be exercised in order to interpret just what was going on.

It is significant to note that in 1952 a mimeographed manuscript was cleared for a very limited circulation to a selected group of more advanced thinkers, to aid them in the evaluation of various events which might otherwise be mysterious and confusing. "It is not released for general distribution," stated an introductory paragraph, "and those who receive it will please use discretion in passing it on."

This mimeographed manuscript, titled "THE FLYING SAUCERS," contained the "by-line" of "Rolf Telano, Tk. Com." It also contained the credit of being "transcribed" by a Borderland Sciences Research Associate, a member of the remarkable West Coast organization founded by the late Meade Layne. The manuscript obviously consisted mainly of communications received by the anonymous associate from one or more space races, which lived mainly on etheric levels different from our plane.

Since the date of its publication much illuminating material, consisting of somewhat similar communications, have been published, but never, in our own opinion, with such clarity and meaning as contained in "THE FLYING SAUCERS." The B.S.R.A. associate probably exercised wisdom in avoiding wide publication of the material. Flying saucer research was in its infancy. Only a few at that time were capable of evaluating such material and accepting it without fear and with feet on the ground.

At long last this material is herein released to UFO students and researchers generally. The saucer situation has changed. Saucers are more than ten years older, and so are their enthusiasts. In those ten years UFO students have heard and read most every theory it would seem possible to expound. Instead of greater understanding of the mystery, we believe, that, contrariwise, even more confusion reigns than in 1952. The clarity of the Telano communications may convey a ring of truth which could dispel some of that confusion. And to the most of us, who were active researchers in 1952, it may give a lump in the throat, and a little added enthusiasm which may have been lost during the intervening, and confusing years.

Most of the Borderland Sciences Associates knew that the name, "Rolf Telano," was that by which the space communicators knew the man who was actually Ralph M. Holland, a member of the engineering profession who lived in Cuyahoga Falls, Ohio. Ralph, whom we never met, but corresponded with frequently, also published a little "magazine," titled "A VOICE FROM THE GALLERY," in which he dealt with such matters as flying saucers, Fortean events, and other "borderline" thought.

Ralph never did explain to me whether his communications with space people were done in trance -- or by what method. However he did it, it was a well kept secret. He once did write me that he was "psychic as a bed post."

Publishing details had cut into our personal correspondence, and I hadn't heard from Ralph in about a year when, very recently, his sister informed me of his death which occurred on

January 26, 1962. I was shocked and saddened by losing a dear friend, and disappointed that we would no longer have him around to prick the bubbles of dogmatic scientific theories and various forms of intellectualism.

I knew, however, that he had departed on a much greater quest than he had pursued in this life -- an exploration of the great beyond, where he would indeed be no stranger, having delved intimately into it from this side.

This "other side" would, I knew, already be quite shaken up, with its inhabitants pulling their intellectual hair -- for Meade Layne, founder of the B.S.R.A., had preceded Ralph there. Ralph, I knew, would be causing additional excitement. For no doubt sacred cows also graze on the fields of other dimensions, other lives and other worlds. No doubt there are ruling intellectual authorities on every plane who need shaking up a bit. No doubt Ralph M. Holland is up to his old tricks "over there."

Few people who read this with interest need fear greatly the transformation we call "death," nor regret the departure from the friends of this plane. Especially, considering the growing population of our departed friends in the great beyond. Such great people as Meade Layne and Ralph Holland will be there. And Dr. M. K. Jessup will be lecturing; saucer students "over there" will still be confusing the two Wilkins' -- H. T. and H. P., both now of that side. Arthur Constance will be no doubt finding they have an "inexplicable sky" there also. And, who knows, perhaps Edward Ruppelt will be running the other-worldly "Project Blue-book"!

The publication of this manuscript of former limited circulation will serve, we hope, as a kind of living memorial to "Rolf Telano. Tk. Com.," and to the man who was known by that name by his communicators.

I believe it will give you a fresh new look at the saucer mystery, and will give you new assurance that, as you look up hopefully at the stars, someone is, indeed, LOOKING DOWN!

Gray Barker
1963

CONTENTS

IN MEMORIAM

Ralph Merridette Holland passed away Friday morning, January 26th, 1962, about 6:30 A. M. with a sudden heart attack (massive occlusion).

He was born in Youngstown, Ohio, August 29, 1899, and lived there until 1914 when the family moved to Akron, Ohio. He attended public school in both Akron and Youngstown, but left school at the age of 16 to start to work. He continued his education at night school, and after working at the engineering profession for years did finally receive his degree.

An avid reader all his life, he was really a self-educated man. Besides becoming tops in his own profession of engineering, he also was very well versed in many other varied fields: law, parliamentary procedures, electronics, unknown or super-natural events, to name a few. He was able to render a decision in law, or fix the TV or washing machine, or build a cupboard with equal skill.

His first job after leaving school was for a German language newspaper in Akron, then he worked for the Akron Beacon Journal (in the plant) but seemed to get a bit of newspaper fever in his blood which stayed with him. While in Detroit, Michigan, he studied journalism and became a free lance reporter, and still kept his press card and credentials after returning home, sending out many stories to wire services and magazines, sometimes under a pen name.

After his brief stint with the Akron Beacon Journal, he started on his career in the engineering profession at the B. F. Goodrich Rubber Company. He worked at several different companies as an engineer in this vicinity, feeling such changes were an advantage to his professional career. Finally he was sent to Scotland by a local rubber company to help set up a rubber plant in that country.

He returned home where the familh had been living since 1920, then went to Detroit to work as an engineer for the Detroit Edison Company. He worked here for approximately five years, returning once again to the family home in 1931. He started to work for the Vaughn Machinery Company here in Cuyahoga Falls in 1932 as an engineer, and was still working there until the time of his death.

As a very young boy, his reading took him into many fields that influenced his life in many ways. He was particularly fond of stories in the science, or science fiction fields. He also started as a stamp collector while living in Youngstown and continued this hobby also. He added another hobby which he also loved very much, that of colored movies. Also the joy of travel, which was carefully recorded in color. In fact he already had our next vacation partially planned for June, with mileage and stops already set up for many days of the trip. Traveling with him was never any problem, for almost every detail had been anticipated by his plans months in advance of any trip.

His quest for the unknown was always a challenge to him. He constantly was in search for the truth, sorting fact from fake, before he would pass the information on. He published a booklet called "A Voice From the Gallery" for many years which included many unusual or out of the way stories or events. He was a member of the Borderland Sciences Research Associates for a number of years, as well as many other groups of a similar nature. He had a host of friends from his long association in this field. He was interested in our own life beyond our earthly one, as well as life on other planets, flying saucers, etc., ever searching for the truth.

He was a Christian long before he joined the Methodist Church here in Cuyahoga Falls. He had always lived his beliefs in his every day life. He never married, and so lavished his affections on his family, being a devoted son and brother.

No one knows the full extent of his generosity in money and talent to try to better someone else's station in life, for his works were done behind the scene -- not for public praise. His efforts might be directed toward the betterment of our own community, or to aid some missionary in far away lands. Or the pushing of himself at work beyond his physical strength in an effort to get work out to the shop so men would not be laid off.

Some people felt he was aloof -- he was always rather quiet and shy in person, but always ready to assist wherever needed, and surely he must have touched, and been an influence, upon a great many lives. For he had the great ability to express himself in writing -- perhaps much better than in person -- and he had a host of friends all over the world.

He always had a great sense of what was right and wrong and the courage (which seems rare these days) to stand up for what he considered to be right. In all his contacts he felt the rights of all were of equal importance and he had the courage and wisdom to carry out those things he felt to be best for all concerned. No one can truthfully say anything ill of him. The world is surely a better place for his having been here, and would be a much better place if there were more like him.

After Ralph died I expressed regret to many people that my brother could not see the many letters of appreciation and praise that have come since his death. How happy it would have made him.

Then I received one letter from one of his friends which said that a few years ago she and another friends had expressed similar regrets to Ralph and that my brother had answered, "Where-ever he is, he DOES know and likes it."

                              --Dora G. Holland

THE FLYING SAUCERS

by Rolf Telano, Tk. Com.

The following information has been cleared for a very limited distribution to a selected group of more advanced thinkers, to aid them in the evaluation of various events which might otherwise be mysterious and confusing. It is not released for general distribution, and those who receive it will please use discretion in passing it on.

(1): There are very ancient laws which declare all intelligent entities, on every planet and plane, and of whatever form, to be brothers; and to make each responsible for his brother's welfare.

Under this law, the higher races assume the obligation of aiding the material, mental, moral, and scientific development of all lesser races with whom they come in contact. The Adamic races of this planet have been under observation by, and have been receiving aid from, various of these higher races ever since their beginnings. Some members of their guardian races have been incarnated among them. Others have come here from other places, using for transport various craft which are now popularly, but incorrectly, grouped under the designation of "flying saucers."

(2): Just prior to World War II, it was noted that certain sinister forces were gaining sonsiderable influence, and were likely to create a very dangerous unbalance between scientific and ethical progress. Scientific knowledge with a high potential of harm was being revealed and pushed rapidly forward before moral development had advanced to a point where such knowledge could be popularly employed. Observation and other activities were sharply stepped up to counter this trend.

(3): An even greater increase in activity was made with
the premature discovery of nuclear fission, which represents a
very great menace to all entities on all planes, and "flying saucers" began to be seen much more frequently than before. The results of the present uncontrolled heavy metals atomic explosions, while
very annoying, are not particularly dangerous except from the stand-
point of atmospheric contamination.

It is possible, however, to employ methods which will re-
act with certain constituents of this planet, and thus cause its
destruction. The present band of asteroids between Mars and Jup-
iter are the remains of a former planet which was destroyed by
this means. The result was catastrophic on all planets and planes.
This particular formula has not yet been discovered on your planet,
and it has been determined that it shall not be developed.

(4): Contrary to the dire warnings of certain cults and
certain astral dwellers, however, there is no desire or intention
of destroying your planet. Neither is there any wish or intent
to depopulate it. Not only is killing forbidden by laws, but also
it is fully recognized that the discarnation of an undesirable
entity affords only temporary relief at best, and may ultimately
aggravate the problem.

Once they have been reoriented on another plane, they
have even greater powers than before and hence greater power for
harm. Any individual discarnations of your people will be only as
a last desperate temporary resort, after all other means have
failed. Remember that our aim is to aid you, not to harm you.

(5): The present situation might well be analogized by
saying that, when a child reaches a certain age, it must be taught
to employ such useful aids as fire and sharp edged tools. It must
be watched, however, and perhaps at times even forcibly restrained,
to prevent it, in its ignorance, from cutting its own throat or
burning the house down. At the moment, the child has just discovered some things far beyond its ability to understand or safely
use.

The situation is further complicated by the fact that some
of its more demonic playmates are urging it to use its new-found
knowledge in particularly dangerous ways. These consist both of
entities on the lower astral, and persons of low intelligence who
inhabit the cavern homes of the ancient Elder Races, and have use
of electronic apparatus which was abandoned there.

(6): It is clearly recognized that the only safe solution
for all concerned is education which will raise the mass intelligence and ethical level of the Adamic races. Restraints cannot be
permanently effective, for some will eventually evade them.

Taboos against the use of the things which have been pre-
maturely learned are worse than useless. Previous experience
indicates that, due to some psychological perversity of the Adamic
races, this tends merely to glamorize the forgidden things and
makes them even more determined than ever to do it. Even temporary
restraints can be employed only with great discretion. One learns
primarily by his own experience and error. These educational errors must be permitted, and restraints should be used only when
they threaten to become major tragedies.

(7): In the final analysis, no one can "teach" another.
One can merely place information before another, in proper sequence,
and in accord with the student's mental capacity and understanding,
and then, by various psychological stratagems, attempt to secure
its acceptance as fact. Fear is a powerful stimulus, and frequently used to channel thought into some desired field. It too
must be used with very great discretion. If fear is permitted to
become too widespread, or too intense, then the fearful ones may,
by the unconscious use of the laws of thought, create the very
thing which they fear. Some news suppressions may have been the
result of stupidity and/or lack of understanding on the part of
your scientists and public officials. Others have been directed
in order to reduce some fear which was getting out of control.

(8): The task of your guardian races is threefold. FIRST
and foremost is to accelerate the spiritual awakening, and the
resulting ethical and moral development of the Adamic races.
SECOND is to closely watch their scientific progress, aiding that
which is beneficial, retarding that which is detrimental, and tem-
porarily halting that which is disastrous. THIRD is to watch the
evil influences which may prompt some to take harmful actions.

Interference with these influences will come only if they
threaten to cause very great harm. The Adamic races must learn to
recognize and resist these influences on their own behalf. To this
end, they must be permitted to make errors in judgment in these
matters, and to suffer the natural consequences thereof, that
they may learn by their own unpleasant experiences.

(9): These three different tasks are being handled by
three different groups, each of which ordinarily restrict their
activities to their own particular task. They work in close har-
mony and cooperation, however, and will promptly aid one another
of the need arises. Each also receives valuable aid from many different groups and individuals on many different planes, including
some of the more advanced thinkers of your own plane. These latter,
either knowingly or unknowingly, often are of great assistance as
the "eyes" and "hands" of those from other planes who cannot work
directly on this one.

(10): Since the ethical and moral phases of the task

involve the use of the mental sciences, they are directed by those who are the recognized masters of these scientices, namely: The Etheric Atlans and Lemuians. Both of these formerly dwelt on the material* plane of your planet, and are now on the etheric counterpart of your planet. On rare occasions they may use some form of mechanical transport, but usually function by non-mechanical means Most of the "flying saucers" seen by you belong to others.

(11): The scientific phases are in the hands of the Etheric Nors, specifically a sub-branch known as the "Viknors." They are the recognized masters of the physical sciences, and for Many ages past it has been the custom of the other races to call upon them for aid in scientific matters. One group of them also formerly inhabited the material plane of your planet, but for a much shorter period of time than the two other races. They are now on Mars and Venus Etheria, with the greater part of those who are engaged in the present operations coming from the latter place. Most of the "flying saucers" are operated by them.

(12): The third phase, that of coping with the evil influences, is handled by a mixed group. Actual direction is in the hands of the Lemuians, with the Nors functioning when anything of a mechanical nature is involved. Much work is also done by the more advanced groups in the caverns, and by groups on the various astral planes.

* * * * * *

(13): Effective observation and action on any plane can be accomplished only on that plane. Thus the flying saucers of the Venusian Nors must be capable of both inter-planetary and inter-plane travel. They must be brought here from Venus, and converted to the vibrational level of this plane. Any of the various types of craft which you have seen could be transported here individually, if desired. Any of them could also be converted to your vibrational frequency individually, either by the use of their own mechanism, or by external influences.

As a matter of operational convenience, however, they are usually brought here in large numbers on a carrier craft. These carriers, by the use of their own mechanism, can teleport themselves to this planet, and simultaneously convert to the desired vibrational level. They remain high above the surface of your planet, in order to prevent detection, and act as a base and coordinating center for their smaller fliers.

(14): In the teleportation method of transportation, the craft and everything on it are converted into pure energy, which is reconverted into its original form at the desired point an almost immeasurable instant later. The control is very deilicate, and it is very difficult to exactly place the craft when working from a mobile control. Due to very slight errors, several car-

riers have been reconverted quite close to the surface of your
planet, and it is believed that at least one of these was obser-
ved from the surface. To avoid such incidents in the future,
the reconversion point is now a considerable distance from your
planet, and the carrier then comes in to the desired altitude by
what you would term "normal space flight."

(15): There are several types of carriers, but the only
one so far used in the present operations is known as the "Voku"
class.** It is about 7,000 feet long and about 500 feet in diameter. It normally carries a crew of about 2,500, including the
technicians and the pilots of the smaller fliers. They can use
several different types of propulsion, according to circumstances.
They are heavily armed.

(16): The smaller fliers use several different types of
proplusion. A form of jet propulsion, although very ancient, is
still extensively used. A very small "dis" ray, playing upon a
stream of fuel in a closed chamber, atomically disintegrates it.
The usual fuel is air, which is collected in scoops by the forward motion of the craft, and automatically compressed to injec-
tion pressure. Other fuels, including metals, can be used in air-
less locations. The end products of the process are radio-active,
and can be detected by means of usual test apparatus. Since none
of the heavy metals group is ever used for fuel, however, the
radioactivity is very short-lived, and does not cause any permanent atmospheric contamination.

(17): Electro-magnetic drive operates by cutting the
natural magnetic lines of force produced by a planetary body, and
can be used only relatively near the surface of some planet. When
used at low altitudes, it has the effect of "blanking out" radio
apparatus, and causing variations in magnetic compasses and other
magnetic apparatus in the vicinity.

(18): "Primary drive" is a true space drive, and, although it can be used on a planet, it is ordinarily used only when
it is desired to travel at a very high rate of speed for a long
distance. Control mechanism on the craft is placed in synchronous
frequency with the universal energy flows which exist in all space,
but just slightly out of phase with them.

Either "lagging" or "leading" phase can be used, depending
upon whether it is desired to travel with the flows, or against
them. The speed depends on the degree of phase angle which, in
turn, depends on the amoung of "shading power" which the control
apparatus can apply. The maximum potential speed is never realized,
since practical navigation and control problems usually limit the
top usable speed to about 27,000 miles per hour. A few exception-
ally skilled pilots have exceeded this.

(19): In addition to the three types of propulsion listed, all craft have means of hovering motionless when desired. One piece of apparatus produces a cone-shaped electrical field which diverts the flow of "gravity" around the craft; much as an umbrella diverts rain, thus cancelling most of the "weight." Another produces a downward electron beam jet which compensates for the slight remaining "weight." It is quite common to use the diversion field while in flight, in order to reduce the amount of power required to maintain flight. This field will, under certain conditions, produce a corona discharge which will give the craft the appearance of being surrounded by a luminous or fiery envelope. A similar corona effect is also quite common on craft using the electromagnetic form of propulsion.

(20): the Viknors have, to date, used seven different types of fliers:

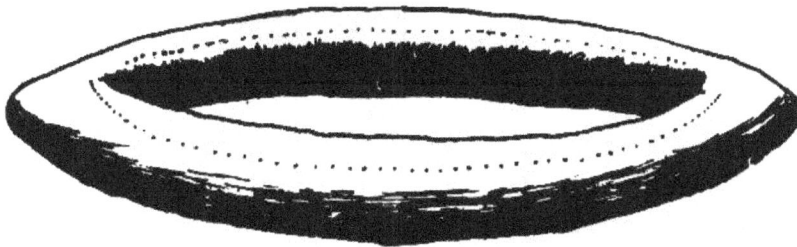

"SUZA CLASS"

These are "doughnut" shaped, about 125 feet outside diameter, with a "hole" about 25 feet in diameter, and about 30 feet thick. They are sometimes referred to as "flying laboratories," because of the large amount of test equipment they carry. They are observation craft, and used only when very involved technical observations are required. Normal crew: 50. Electromagnetic drive.

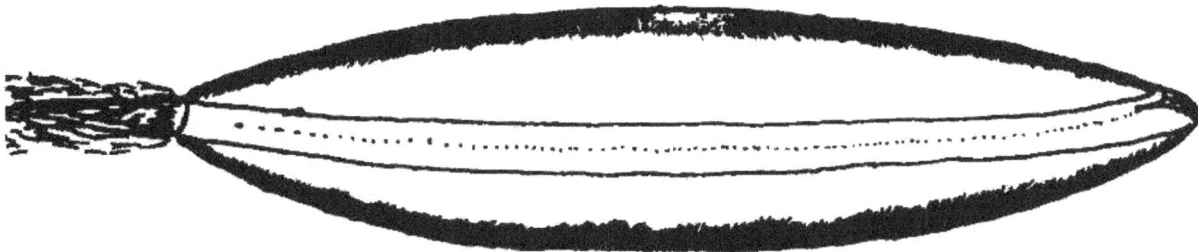

"TONTON" CLASS

Cigar shaped, about 100 feet long by 25 feet maximum diameter. Primarily an escort and fighter craft. Used only if circumstances require protection for the other craft. Normal crew: 20. Uses both jet and primary drive.

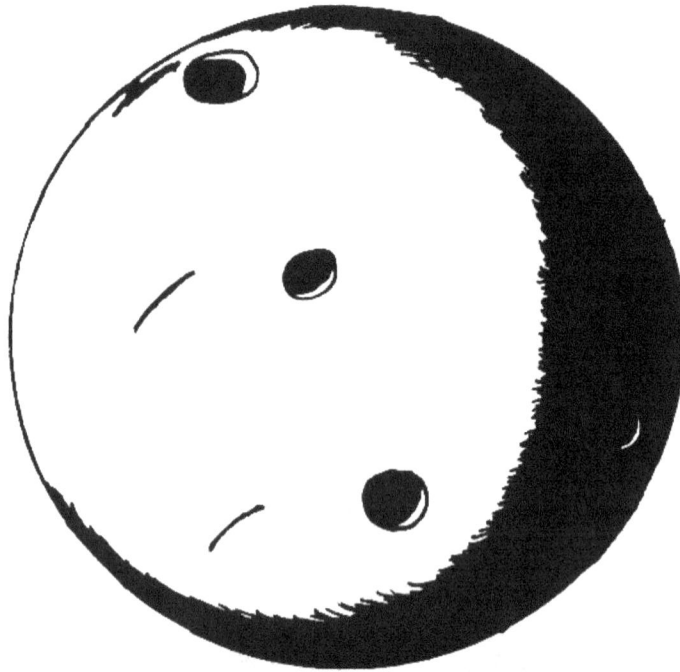

"FAKLE TYPE"

Spherical, about 100 feet in diameter. A transport craft, used to carry both passengers and cargo. Normal crew: 25 or 30. Electromagnetic drive.

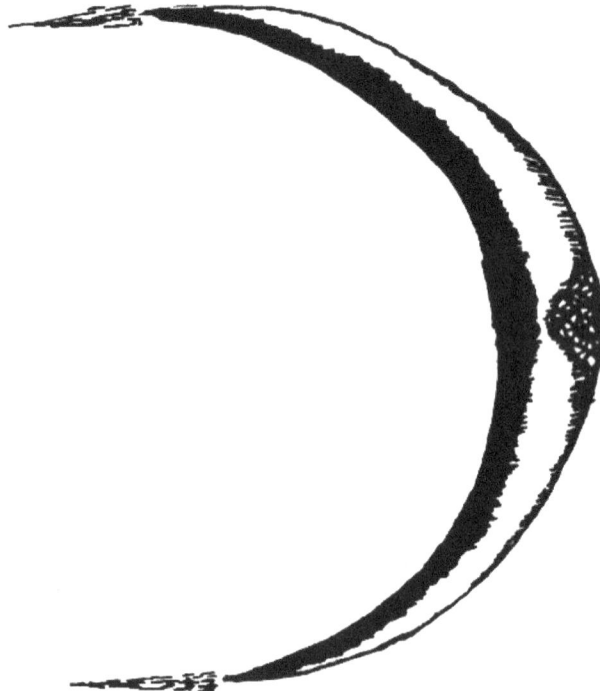

"OLON TYPE"

Crescent or "rubber heel" shaped, about 45 feet across by 18 feet thick. Reconnaissance craft. Normal crew: 5. Uses jet drive, one jet being placed in a universal mounting at each of the points of the crescent. Control is by changing the direc-

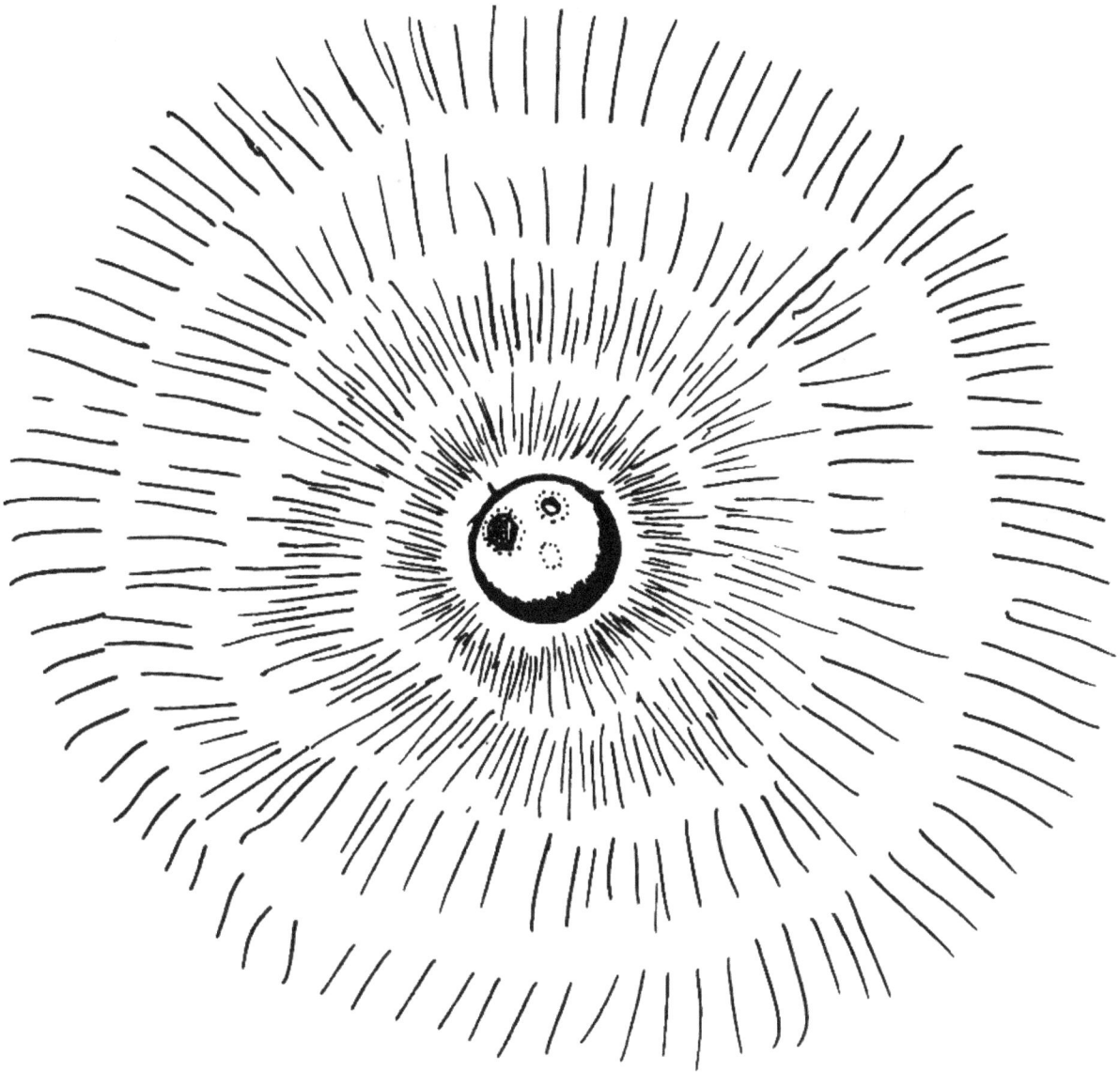

"POMIDER" TYPE

A smaller version of the "Pomid" (see next page), being
only about one foot in diameter. Frequently mistaken for a "fire
ball."
****

A note about these drawings: These pictorial represen-
tations of the text were made by Joe Gonzales, local UFO student   .
and press operator at Saucerian Publications. He drew them after
studying the text and trying to visualize Rolf Telano's impressions.
He does not claim that they are "psychic" impressions or actual
drawings of the craft described, but the editor believes that the
author would have been highly satisfied with them had he been living
to see them. These drawings did not appear in the original manuscript, and are interjected to help the reader visualize an approx-
imation of the craft described by Telano. -- G.B.

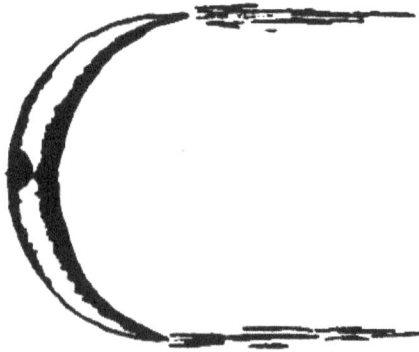

"OLONER" TYPE

     Similar in shape and construction to the "Olon" type, but much smaller, being only about 14 feet across. A "single place" flier, but can carry two when required.

"POMID" TYPE

     Spherical, about 5 or 6 feet in diameter. Robot and remote controlled from some other craft. Used for visual observation where larger craft would attract too much attention. Electro-magnetic drive.

     (21): Aside from the Viknor craft described, various other types are seen at very infrequent intervals. Some groups on your planet and plane have found and reactivated very ancient fliers which were left here by the old "Elder Races." These are mostly predecessors of the "Olon" class. Visitors from other solar systems occasionally come to this one for various purposes. If their purpose is not malicious, they are permitted to proceed. Otherwise

they are usually intercepted and turned back in the outer limits
of this solar system.

(22): The craft most deserving of the name "flying saucers" were brought to this planet in 1949 by a midget race from
your moon.*** These were slightly less than 100 feet in diameter,
but much of this area was areo-dynamic surface, the actual cabin
being only about 16 feet diameter. They used an electro-magnetic,
or "earth induction" drive, but different in construction than that
used by the Nor craft. It was their first inter-planetary flight,
and their purpose was peaceful exploration. They became stranded
here, without base or supervisory control, when the carrier craft
became disabled. The small fliers were unable to return to Luna,
because they were incapable of space flight.(Ed. Note: Could this have

provided the basis for the story of the crashed saucer related by
Frank Scully in his book, "BEHIND THE FLYING SAUCERS"? This and
other "crashes" have been related by various sources. Readers may
remember the rash of strange close-up sightings occurring around
this time, and particularly later, in 1952. If Telano's information
is valid, the stranded saucers and the search for survivors by
Viknor carrier, may well be the explanation for most of these
sightings. -- G.B.)

(23): One of the Lunar fliers was shot down over northern
Mexico by the over-anxious pilot of a Nor patrol craft, when it
failed to respond to signals, or otherwise identify itself. Several
others were caused to crash by radar, to which they were particularly susceptible because of the insufficient shielding of their drive

and control apparatus. As soon as it became apparent that the r.-turn of their carrier would be indefinitely delayed, and that the craft and pilots were unable to cope with conditions on this planet, they were rounded up and returned to Luna by a Viknor carrier. Of the original 37 fliers, 26 were safely returned to their home base. Eight are known to have crashed. It is assumed that the remaining 3 went down unnoticed

- - - - - - - - - -

*The word "material is used as a matter of convenience to indicate your particular vibrational plane. It is, of course, technically incorrect, since all other planes are also "material," usually more so than this one, but merely on a different frequency.

**The class names of the various craft listed are the nearest English spellings of the actual phonetic names.

***The atmosphere and water on Luna and, consequently, the life, is mainly concentrated on the far side, which is never seen from your planet. The conditions is analagous to a bucket of water being whirled at the end of a rope, with the water being held at the far end by the action of centrifugal force. Expeditions have come to the near side to attempt to signal Earth on several occasions. In several instances the signals were seen by your astronomers, but were ignored because of their firm belief that Luna was lifeless.

Rolf Telano, Tk. Comm.

COMMENTS OF THE YADA DI SHI'ITE
================================

(Editor's Note: The Yada Di Shi'ite is one of the Mark
Probert trance "controls," or entities who speak through Probert
while the remarkable medium is in trance state. Communication
with these controls formed the basis of most of the theory and
philosophy advanced by the Borderland Sciences Research Associates
while under the direction of the late Meade Layne. The Mark Probert controls stated that most flying saucers were etheric craft,
materializing on our "plane" from a higher one. -- G.B.)

On January 24, 1952, the document signed Rolf Telano,
received by BSR Associate R.M.H., was read to the Tibetan control
Yada di Shi'ite, Mark Probert being in deep trance at the time.
The object, of course, was to obtain the comments, either pro or
contra, of this highly respected communicator, with whom we have
been in almost weekly contact for nearly five years. Since there
has always been a basic agreement among the 15 communicators of
this group, we feel reasonably certain that statements by the Yada
have the support of other members of the group as well. I quote
the substance of his comments only:

"I see no reason why this communication from your Associate R. H., known also as Rolf Telano, should not be made public,
since a few will profit by it and others will not be harmed. It
should, however, be presented with the utmost circumspection.

"First of all, your readers should bear in mind that the
situations and events with which the R. T. communication deals are
highly complex and relate not only to your planet but in various
ways to the entire solar system. Precise and exact statements
concerning matters of such magnitude are almost impossible and
should be taken with reserve -- not as being wrong, but as nece-
ssarily inadequate.

"Approaching with this attitude of mind, I find no serious
--29--

errors in the document you have read to me.

"Concerning the 'Etheric Atlans and Lemuians ... both of whom formerly dwelt on your planet and are now on the etheric counterpart of your planet' (Paragraph 10), do not take this as implying that entire races enter the etheric directly after leaving earth life. But many individuals can and do enter the etheric worlds, according to their personal status and destiny. The statement about the etheric NORS is correct, again with reference to a group.

"I have no knowledge of any construction work in the caverns or of any craft issuing from that source." (Note: this is the sole point on which the Yada showed pronounced skepticism -- M. L.) (Paragraph 12)

"The data about the carrier craft is essentially correct (Paragraphs 13-15). And the reconversion mentioned, of these craft, to the vibrational level of your plane, is one important cause of the explosions in the atmosphere and others.

"The expression 'heavily armed' should not be taken as meaning, against yourselves. Yes, it is true that there is something like a policing of your planet and of the entire solar system. Yes, the statement about 'guardian races,' their purposes, duties and so on, (Paragraphs 1-9) is essentially correct. Your visitors truly wish you well and desire to help you and protect you. Is it wise to meet them with fear and with hostility?

"Well, 27,000 miles an hour is not very fast!" (Note: that this speed refers to our vibrational level, not to crossing interplanetary distances, which is accomplished by other means -- M. L.)

"Concerning the Moon, etc. (Paragraph 22): There is no race which permanently inhabits the Moon. But the Moon has been used for ages (on its 'dark side') as a meeting ground, for scientific work, and for many meetings of occult or secret Orders. Yes, signals have been sent to your earth from the moon...The incidents described (accidents to the Lunar flight, the help by the Viknor carrier, etc.,) actually occurred.

"The huge craft called Kareeta (fall of 1946) over San Diego, came from the moon."

(Editor's note: This is the end of the comments by the Yada Di-Shi'ite, who has described himself, during different communications, as an Oriental who lived 500,000 years ago in an ancient civilization in the Himalayas. He was a priest in the temple there, was killed when an earthquake destroyed the Yu civilization. -- G.B.)

LETTER FROM "ROLF TELANO"

(Editor's Note: The material in the original published manuscript was not organized as one would expect to see in a magazine article, a book, or a thesis. In re-publishing it the Editor makes no attempt to change the format, even at the risk of some repetition.

For example, here are appended excerpts from a letter received subsequent to the interview with the Control, the Yada di Shi'ite, summarized on preceding pages. The letter is from Associate R. M. H. (Rolf Telano), addressed to Meade Layne, BSRA Director, and dated January 21, 1952. -- G.B.)

The group on Venus Etheria, from whom the Disc information came, have removed all restrictions on its publication. To quote their exact words, "He can tell it to any who will listen." The impression seemed to be, that not too many would listen...The restrictive introductory paragraph should of course be eliminated ...along with any other details of no probable interest to the readers. So far as I am concerned, the more the merrier. One cannot view these things from too broad a viewpoint or consider too many different sources, since any and all may be valuable.

As to its origin: It came from a group on Venus Etheria who are directly concerned with the mission on this planet and plane, and they have no objection to having the fact known. Different ones contributed various thoughts and bits of information, but I simply put them all together. Those to whom direct credit is due are:

Gerald Peterson, a kind of Chief of Operations of the various craft here. He supplied the data regarding the different varieties of craft used.

Ollie Rolson, Technical Officer, supplied data on means of driving the craft.

Portia Norton, a historian, supplied various historical data.

Mira Peterson, various psychological comments.

Nels Gordon, a sort of interplane communications officer, who gave the data on the earth Etherians and various astral planes.

Borealis Telano, a Priestess, who made various ethical comments.

These are all Etherians and their names would probably add nothing to the value of the published information, but are listed for any possible future use. (NOTE: These appear to be former earth people now functioning on etheric levels. They are not members of an Etheric race -- who do not incarnate on our planet, as I understand it. The terms etheric and etheria cover immense regions of life, thought, and space. The relation of these etheric humans to the "true" Etherians is as yet unknown. See further note on this, next section. M. L.)

The name Rolf Telano is actually the name by which I am known to the Venusian Etherians, and also a name known to many of the BSR Associates. The only real objection I have to the use of my real name (R.H.) is that so many insist on thinking that, because I happen to know a little about something, I must know all about everything ... and get mad or feel hurt and accuse me of holding out on them.

Of possible interest to you personally -- at the high point last year there were four carriers here, each of which carries approximately 150 small flyers of various types. Only a part of them was in use at any one time, and some were special service types which are seldom used. At present only one carrier, the Trass Voku, is on duty. The others, however, are available for instant recall if needed.

Again, I shall be quite interested in the reaction and comment of the Mark Probert Controls. Their point of view will, of course, be that of the ethereal or upper astral plane of this planet -- and it is possible that they might see some things in a different light than we do. It has never been my privilege to meet any of this group, since my work does not bring me into contact with them; but various of my friends and companions on Venus Etheria have a very high opinion of their motives and judgment.

Yours, etc. RMH -- Rolf Telano

(Further Notes by the Editor): The reader cannot be urg·ɩ
too strongly to read this material most carefully, and to note iɩs
proper sequence. Most of this material was published and sent out
to BSRA members at different times, to be added to the Rolf Telano
Communications file.

Read carefully and understood, the material forms a grad-
ual development of etheric theory in regard to the visitations
óf so many UFOs in 1952 and earlier.

The reader is also urged to emulate the various people
and entities who comment, and thus not to jump to immediate con-
clusions; but instead to realize that generalities and approxi-
mations are being developed in order to approach a complete
understanding of the Saucer phenomena.

Never does Rolf Telano, Meade Layne, nor the various
entities involved try to give you complete answers. In fact
the entities state rather clearly that they are not telling us
everything -- for the simple fact that we could not understand
it even if they did so.

Our personal opinion is that one of the main faults with
UFO research has been the endeavor to completely explain it in
one framework or theory. -- G.B.

FURTHER NOTE ON HUMANS IN ETHERIA

By Meade Layne

The important matter involved here is not the almost hope-less attempt to define an "etheric" plane or world, and to distin-guish it from the Astral, Montal, "Spiritual," and so on -- but the fact that the control of at least some of the visiting craft is in the hands of human beings who formerly lived on earth.

This partly clears up several perplexing instances of small craft landing in remote places, and containing normal-appear-ing human beings. Such cases have led to the far-too-hasty con-clusion that all the visiting craft were of terrestrial origin.

We have repeatedly urged the consideration that these happenings have an infinite variety -- in form, in size, in means of propulsion, and in purposes.

People who get no other exercise than jumping to conclus-ions, should all be accomplished gymnasts by this time.

The Director has been writing on this subject for five years and has encountered a great number of facts which seemed in-consistent and contradictory. He long ago abandoned hope of any single, intelligible solution.

The information given by the Mark Probert Controls in the fall of 1946, seems to be basically correct in the light of all future developments. They have never attempted (quite wisely, no doubt) to cover all phases and angles of the phenomena which spread out over the whole solar system and have been going on for many thousands of years. It is "no news" to them, and they get a little bored with our agitation of the subject.

Planetary isolation is as stupid and impossible as the

isolation of a race, a State, a community, or an individual. There are planetary responsibilities. There is a practical rule or law of Help-and-Harm-Not which obtains even between the galaxies. There are Guardian Races who help and protect us, and could do more for us IF we had the sense to accept and understand -- Our "scientific achievements" are the toys of children, compared with those of other humans, elsewhere --

The visitation of the ether ships opens immense perspectives, not only in the positive sciences, but in all fields of human· thought: Art, religion, philosophy, ethics, morals, human conduct and powers and resources, a revaluation of values.

Is our generation capable of even beginning this learning process? Will the Impossibles have to be removed -- and how? Let us concern ourselves with only two things: to learn more, understand more, and to help other people when we can. But the nation, the race, the planet move toward their own destinies and cannot be hindered.

We have sent you what might be called the most remarkable news release in twenty centuries! But is it "news" at all, if it is not accepted, not even known, not understood, not believed in? Is a comet great news to the moles, or a symphony among peacocks?

Let us remember that Rolf Telano is writing of the DISCS for the most part, and of the Etheric double of Venus, and of humans living there -- and that most of this type of craft come from this source (as the Mark Probert Controls said long ago). But there is a swarm of other craft in our skies, utterly fantastic, many of them. Are the monitors of these, excarnate humans also? I think not -- not all of them, anyhow.

NOTES BY BOREALIS TELANO

The following material was sent to BSRA subsequent to the mimeographing and sending out of the previous material herein reprinted. It was received by Rolf Telano after inquiries of various sorts were sent to him by Meade Layne concerning the previous communications. "I pass it along for what it may be worth to you," Telano wrote to Meade Layne. -- G.B.

****

(By Communicator Borealis Telano)

These matters are much too complicated to be dealt with on a part time basis. You had best stick to your own job and not bother your head too much with such affairs, however....

(A) The words "planes," "Etherians," "Earthians," and so on, are rather ill-advised althouth they are occasionally used as a matter of convenience. In the minds of most people, however, they build up too much of a picture of definite places, with fixed boundaries -- and perhaps even a customs and immigration service.

(B) All planes are actually one. There is merely a continuously increasing vibrational frequency, beginning with the "sub-physical" and rising through the "physical," "Astral" and "Etheric" to the final and original Source. Entities simply gravitate to some particular height on the scale, according to their individual desires and mental abilities. The lower ranges, from and to which the dwellers successively incarnate and discarnate to and from the "physical" are usually called the "Astral" planes. The upper ranges, where such return to the lower physical is rare, are commonly referred to as the "Etherics." All divisions are arbitrary. None can say where the upper Astral stops and the lower Etheric begins. All names and designations are artificial inventions, and have only as much meaning as the individual user assigns to them.

--37--

(C) All entities on all planes were probably on the physical of some planet or other, at some time, though it may have been countless eons ago in some cases. Therefore, all are probably former "Earthians" in the strict technical sense. The higher one rises on the vibrational scale, the thinner becomes the cord which binds them to earthy or physical things. Eventually they reach a point where all connection with the "physical" is, for all practical purposes, broken. Their thoughts and interests are along entirely different lines, and they have no desire to return to the physical. There is no actual reason why they could not return, if they wished to do so, and there have been cases where some have done so. Perhaps after a few millions or billions of years one can become bored even on Heavi'n!

(D) The particular group which dictated the "Flying Saucer" report dwell on the Etheric, but not on the highest levels. The number who incarnate to the physical is very small, as compared to the total, and even these volunteer for such incarnation mainly from a sense of obligation rather than any personal preference. Their sole motive is to aid the Adamic races of your planet and plane. They can, to a certain degree, function by merely materializing, or converting to the frequency of your plane. Such requires constant mental effort to maintain the proper vibrational frequency, however, and hampers effective total thought to that degree. Therefore a certain number are actually incarnated into earth-born physical bodies, and live out a normal lifetime.

(E) Aside from their obligations under certain cosmic laws, the groups are tied to the Adamic races by the fact that they created them, and are therefore particularly responsible for them. When these groups first came to the physical plane of your planet, they found that their physical bodies were not entirely suited to the environment. In an effort to improve the situation, they began, by selective breeding and cross-breeding, to develop a better adapted physical body. The final choice was the ancestor race of the present Adamic races, which was a cross between the Elder Races themselves and a certain man-like animal native to your planet. This ancestor animal is now extinct. During experimentation these physical forms were inhabited by the KUIS ("spirits") of some of the lower ones among the Elder Races, and certain animal life forms. This is not recognized by your theologies, but every living thing has a KUI (what you would call "soul" or "spirit"), and these Kuis differ only in the degree of their advancement. They can and do evolve in successive incarnations, and can and do ultimately inhabit physical bodies of human form. It would not be advisable to publicise this statement as it would create too much opposition at present.

(D) The intention to incarnate into the bodies of the Adams was abandoned long before they had been developed to a satisfactory point, because the Elder Races had in the meantime learned how to advance themselves to a more suitable vibrational level. The Adams were left behind in their imperfect state, but the members of the former parent races still recognize a special obligation to aid them in their development. (End of dictation by Borealis Telano)

COMMENTS OF LO SUN YAT

On the evening of February 4, 1952, Meade Layne made in-
quiry of the trance Control LO SUN YAT (a Tibetan), speaking through
the mediumship of Mark Probert. The questions referred chiefly to
the subject matter of Paragraphs (C) and (D) of the preceeding
dictation of Borealis Telano, and the substance of the replies was
as follows:

"Yes, there are such Guardian Races, and their responsi-
bility stems from the facts described. This cross-breeding actually
took place, in the dim past, but the race resulting from this union
came to an end with Lemuria...The 'man-like animal native to your
planet' was originally created by the Etheric 'colonizors' ...The
'Cross' was not a true ancestor race, it was a kind of ancestral
pattern resembling man in form. Man originated from a later ex-
periment. In one of their experiments to become one with the
material world, some forms that were made resembled the anthropoid
apes...Yes, there was actual mating between the Etherians and these
earth-animals. 'Sons of God mating with daughters of men' -- a
fine rhetorical statement but not a pretty thing by any means --
if you could only see what they looked like. About the KUIS --
these are the 'servient spirits' of your Huna. Yes, they are a
kind of fragmentation of a human entity. The Higher Mind may for
various reasons leave the Low Self in control of the body. Many
KUIS are now in human bodies. Very many indeed in Asia, Africa,
India. They possess animal instincts only. Those who seem to
have no aura possess the chemical-radiation aura only. One may
say that the KUIS are the lower or the lowest part of the mind.
They are a dissociated part.

"Yes, certainly, there are races of Etheric people who are
now excarnate humans and have never lived on earth. Some of the
'discs' and other sky-craft are truly operated by excarnate earth
people, but some are operated by the 'true' Etherians. They will

C O M M E N T   B Y   T H E   N O R   G R O U P

(Editor's Note: This Comment by the Nor Group, received through Rolf Telano, is in regard to the comment made by the Mark Probert Control Yada di Shi'ite presented on preceeding pages... G.B.)

The Nor Group heartily endorses the note of caution introduced by the Yada, and feels that it cannot be too highly stressed. When the question of releasing the report was being considered, there was considerable discussion as to the dangers inherent in the over-simplification which would be necessary. The attempt to state in a single paragraph things which would take several volumes to properly explain could only result in the broadest possible generalization, and many things would have to be left unsaid. It was decided to risk the danger because those who would read it would probably be the type who were capable of reading between the lines and catching the spirit of what was said, rather than staying within the mere letter of it. The Yada's remarks emphasize this, and serve as a valuable introduction.

(Portia Norton): The Yada's statement is correct. Only the more advanced members of these groups advanced to the etheric. The lower ones remained behind on the physical. There is some evidence that some of them mingled with the early Adams. The others eventually died out.

(Nels Gordon): There seems to be a misunderstanding by the Yada here.* We made no mention of any "construction" in the caverns. So far as we know, there has been none, and it is very unlikely that there will be any. The vast majority of those who dwell there are mentally incapable of such. The few higher groups have few, if any, mechanical inclanations and concentrate most exclusively on the mental sciences. Most of the cavern dwellers;

--43--

even the lower groups; have learned to operate the ancient mechanism, which was abandoned there to some degree, but it is doubtful that any of them could duplicate it.

The fliers mentioned were, according to our information, stored under ground, but those who reactivated them, and are supposedly now using them, could not be properly called "cavern dwellers." They are said to be a certain priestly group from Tibet and, while they have access to the "underworld," they customarily live on the surface. We regard the source of this information as usually reliable, but not infallible. Various members of the Mark Probert Controls, who formerly lived in this area, could check the accuracy of the information better than we.

The Statement regarding "explosions" caused by teleporting is correct. The sudden shifting of the mass results in a violent explosion at the point of departure, and a corresponding explosion at the point of reconversion. For this reason it is customary to set these two points as far as possible from any inhabited planet or plane, and cover the remaining distance by other means of propulsion. But there are occasional errors -- or circumstances may make it impossible at times.

Both the Yada and Meade Layne are correct, in that 27,000 miles is fast only relative to your plane, and other means would be used to accomplish interplanetary or interstellar movement.

(Gerald Peterson): The statement is correct regarding the permanent life forms on Luna at the present time which are of a very low order (mosses and fungi). It is much used, however, as a base by various groups, some of whom are there for considerable lengths of time. Semi-permanent installations are maintained by several of these groups.

The "Kareeta" was a separate undertaking, and not connected with the "Lunar fliers" mentioned in the report. As noted by the Yada, it also used Luna as its base while in this solar system and plane.

Notes on comment by Meade Layne: It is correct that there are many other objects in the sky aside from those mentioned in the report. For the most part, these were more on the order of "visitors" or, in some cases, "tourists," and were here on some specific and, usually, "one time" mission. To list all of them would be next to impossible, even if complete information were at hand, which it is not. Some of the fantastic shapes reported were the results of faulty observations or, in some cases, a mere hoax. One must take care not to swing from the one extreme that "there are no discs" to the other that all reports are automatically correct. Some of them actually did assume fantastic shapes, for reasons best known to themselves. In certain cases, we can deduce the reasons, but it is merely speculation. The report deals with only the Nor craft, which are the most numerous and most frequently seen at the present time.

Notes on comment by Lo Sun Yat (Portia Norton): According to our records, there were many survivors of the destruction of both Mu and Atlan. These consisted of colonists who had gone out from the Motherlands to settle other parts of the planet. There are many discrepancies between the historic records of various peoples, and it would be difficult to determine the correct one. The events took place so long ago that some of the details have become dim, even in the minds of those who were then present.

The absence of the "R" in Lemuia, in the dictated text, was intentional. The Lemuians had no "R" in their alphabet. Neither did their closest descendants, the early Polynesians.

Also, according to our records, the Adams were not the result of the actual mating of the Elder Races and the animal forms, although the original text may cause some confusion on this. They resulted from the artificial merging of the various life cells in laboratories. In many of the experiments, actual mating between the animal forms selected would have been physically impossible. There was, however, some actual mating between the "sons of God" and the results of these experiments at a much later date.

(Borealis Telano): The word "kui" means many things to different people. As used in the original communication it was intended to embrace the entire triune "inner self." It is often difficult for even some of the more advanced individuals to mentally accept the thought that they are actual brother to the beasts. Telepathic contact with the beasts, particularly the higher animal forms, will establish the fact that they vary only in the degree of their advancement. In some cases one is compelled to feel that perhaps the animal is the more advanced of the two!

*(Note by Meade Layne): The misunderstanding by the Yada was due to an awkward phrasing on my part involving the word, "construction." -- M. L.

OTHER BOOKS AVAILABLE FROM SAUCERIAN PUBLICATIONS

ADAMSKI, George: COSMIC PHILOSOPHY (Privately printed book
a available to serious students of Adamski's teachings, $7.00;
FLYING SAUCERS HAVE LANDED, $3.50; INSIDE THE SPACE SHIPS,
$3.95; Adamski's QUESTION AND ANSWERS (Booklet No. 2), 50¢

BARKER, Gray: THEY KNEW TOO MUCH ABOUT FLYING SAUCERS (Auto-
graphed on request), $3.50; THE SAUCERIAN REVIEW (100-page
Review of 1955 Saucerevents), $1.50; Rare Back Issues of
THE SAUCERIAN BULLETIN, 35¢ each.

BENDER, Albert K.: FLYING SAUCERS AND THE THREE MEN, $3.95;
Complete bound file (offset reproduction) of SPACE REVIEW,
$1.50.

BLAVATSKY, H. P.: THE SECRET DOCTRINE (2 Vol.), $7.50; ISIS
UNVEILED (2 Vol.), $7.50; KEY TO THEOSOPHY, $3.50; STUDIES
IN OCCULTISM, $2.50; VOICE OF THE SILENCE, $1.50.

BRANDON, Wilfred: (Brandon is a noted teacher on the etheric
plane. These books dictated through the famous medium,
Edith Ellis) OPEN THE DOOR, $3.00; LOVE IN THE AFTERLIFE,
$3.00; INCARNATION, $3.00; WE KNEW THESE MEN, $3.00.

BROTHER PHILIP: BROTHERHOOD OF THE SEVEN RAYS (SECRET OF THE
ANDES, $3.95.

CAYCE, Edgar: (Books about & Readings of) THE GREAT PYRAMID,
$1.00; GOD'S OTHER DOOR, $1.00; LOST ATLANTIS, $1.50; ONE
HUNDRED QUESTIONS AND ANSWERS, $1.00; MANY MANSIONS by Gina
Cerminara (Based on life readings by Cayce), $4.00; THERE
IS A RIVER (Story of Edgar Cayce), by Thomas Sugrue, $5.00.

DAVID-NEEL, Alexandra: MAGIC AND MYSTERY IN TIBET, $6.00;
INITIATIONS AND INITIATES IN TIBET, $5.00.

DAY, Harvey: THE STUDY AND PRACTICE OF YOGA, $3.75.

FATE MAGAZINE: Most any issue 1953 onward, 35¢ each.

GRANT, Rev. W. V.: MEN IN THE FLYING SAUCERS IDENTIFIED, 50¢;
MEN FROM THE MOON IN AMERICA, 50¢; THE GREAT DICTATOR WHOSE
NUMBER IS 666, 50¢.

HOWARD, Dana: EARTHBORN VENUSIAN, $4.00; DIANE, SHE CAME FROM
VENUS, $3.00; UP RAINBOW HILL, $4.50; KEYS TO THE CITADEL OF
SPACE, $3.95; THE KINGDOM OF SPACE, $2.00.

KEYHOE: THE FLYING SAUCER CONSPIRACY, $3.95; FLYING SAUCERS
FROM OUTER SPACE, $3.95; FLYING SAUCERS: TOP SECRET, $3.95.

KRASPECON, Dino: MY CONTACT WITH FLYING SAUCERS, $3.95.

MENGER, Howard: FROM OUTER SPACE TO YOU, $4.50; MUSIC FROM
ANOTHER PLANET (33 1/3 LP Record), $4.95.

MICHAEL X BOOKS: The following at $2.00 each: "SECRETS OF HIG-
HER CONTACT" (Who are the Space People?); "THE D-DAY SEERS
SPEAK" (A picture of things to come -- in startling Focus);
"RAINBOW CITY AND THE INNER EARTH PEOPLE";"FLYING SAUCER REV-
ELATIONS" (Visitors from Venus and other planets); "THE
SPACEMASTERS SPEAK" (Messages from Space People to People
of Earth); "RELEASE YOUR COSMIC POWERS" (Reveals the Cosmic
Balance Secret); "YOUR PART IN THE GREAT PLAN" (This book

(Continued Reverse Side)

gives important Techniques); "IS HITLER ALIVE--WE WANT YOU)" (The
astonishing escape of Adolph Hitler); "THE WORLD SECRET OF FATIMA"
(What is the earth-shaking secret hidden until now?) "THE SEVEN
GOLDEN PROPHECIES" (As revealed by the Magi, Enoch, Elder Edda,
Merlin). The following at $5.00 each: "VENUSIAN HEALTH MAGIC,"
"VENUSIAN SECRET SCIENCE." (All Michael X Books stiff paper bound)
MICHELET, Jules: SATANISM AND WITCHCRAFT, $3.00 (Soft Bound)
OAHSPE: $10.00.
PHYLOS: A DWELLER ON TWO PLANETS, $7.50.
RAMPA, T. Lobsang: DOCTOR FROM LHASA, $4.50.
NOSTRADAMUS: THE COMPLETE PROPHECIES OF NOSTRADAMUS, $5.00.
SHAVER MYSTERY: Subscription to series of quarterly books
 titled "HIDDEN WORLDS" $6.00 per year, Sample, $1.50.
SHERMAN, Harold: HOW TO USE THE POWER OF PRAYER, $3.95; KNOW
 YOUR OWN MIND, $3.95.
STRANGES, Frank E.: FLYING SAUCERAMA (Contains many photos)$3.00
SUMMERS, Montague: HISTORY OF WITCHCRAFT, $5.00; GEOGRAPHY OF
 WITCHCRAFT, $10.00.
TRENCH, Brinsley Le Poer: THE SKY PEOPLE, $4.50.
      Write us for Flying Saucer or Occult titles not listed
         ****
    OTHER BOOKS IN THIS SERIES SIMILAR TO ONE CONTAINING
         THIS LIST. All Stiff Bound, 60-100 Pages.

"THE BENDER MYSTERY CONFIRMED" Readers of Bender's Works
Comment With their Own Ideas and Experiences. 100 PP $3.00.

"UFO WARNING" By John Stuart. Researcher Meets with startling
and terrifying results. 80 PP $3.00.

"THE FLYING SAUCERS" By Rolf Telano, Tk. Com. Startling
Communications from Space Explaining Saucer Sightings. 45 PP $2.00

"FLYING SAUCERS AND THE FATHER'S PLAN" By Laura Mundo. (April '53)
Mankind is Helped Back to his Original Status by Space People. $3.00

"THE STRANGE CASE OF DR. M. K. JESSUP" Edited by Gray Barker,
(March, 1953). Explores the suicide of UFO author and strange
communications before his death. $3.00

COMING IN THIS SERIES:
"FLYING SAUCERS IN THE BIBLE" No release date set.
"THE FLATWOODS MONSTER" Souvenir Book. No release date set.
"LIFE ON A THOUSAND WORLDS" No release date set.
"THE WORLD OF KAZIK" By Albert K. Bender. No release set.
         ****
Order from: SAUCERIAN BOOKS, Box 2228, Clarksburg, W. Va.

www.ingramcontent.com/pod-product-compliance
Lightning Source LLC
Chambersburg PA
CBHW081204270326
41930CB00014B/3297